Classic Marques

CORVETTE

Classic
Marques

CORVETTE

Ian Penberthy

LONGMEADOW
P R E S S

This 1993 edition published by
Longmeadow Press
201 High Ridge Road
Stamford CT 06904

Produced by
Brompton Books Corporation
15 Sherwood Place
Greenwich CT 06830

ISBN: 0-681-41826-5

Printed in Hong Kong

0 9 8 7 6 5 4 3 2 1

PAGE 1: The 1984-7 Corvette was a sleek-looking automobile. It was a big leap forward from the previous generation of 'vettes, but still carried many unmistakeable Corvette styling clues.

PAGE 2-3: By 1959, the Corvette had come of age and came with engines ranging in power from 245 to 290bhp. The styling excesses of 1958 had been toned down, too, resulting in an attractive, well-rounded package.

THESE PAGES: To celebrate 25 years of Corvette production, Chevrolet offered this Silver Anniversary model in 1978.

Contents

Introduction

At some time in mid-1952, the President of General Motors (GM), Harlow Curtice, and the General Manager of GM's Chevrolet Division, Thomas H. Keating, met with Harley Earl, head of the company's Art & Color Section which was responsible for the design of all new GM products. The purpose was to view a mock-up of a project that Earl and a few trusted members of his design team had been working on in secret, a car that he felt would stimulate Chevrolet sales – which were flagging after the initial post-World War II boom – and add considerable glamor and prestige to what was, it must be said, a fairly unexciting range of family cars.

When Earl raised the curtain, he revealed a sleek, low-slung, two-seat sportscar; something that no other American volume producer had in their line-up, even though there was a definite market for such prestige cars, as demonstrated by the success of such imported European marques as MG, Jaguar and Porsche. Earl was convinced that his baby would see off the foreign competition. Moreover, he argued that it would pull a lot of people into Chevy dealers' showrooms, and while they may have only been there out of curiosity, there was a chance that they could be sold one of the more mundane Chevy lines before they left.

To keep production costs of the new sportscar to a minimum, given that the numbers built were expected to be considerably lower than any of the company's range of

family sedans, Earl proposed the use of many off-the-shelf Chevy parts. Furthermore, the body would be made in a new material that had proved ideal for low-volume production – glass-reinforced plastic (fiberglass). GRP had been used with considerable success in boat construction, and a number of small companies had also produced GRP bodies for fitting to standard sedan chassis and running gear in a bid to meet America's demand for sporting two-seaters. Sadly, none of these had met with any great success due to the mechanical components used and a lack of resources.

GM was ideally placed to resolve both problems, and although the available mechanical components were not all ideal for a sportscar – being sedan-based – with a bit of tinkering here and there they could be made to work well enough. Furthermore, although it probably wasn't considered at the time, development work was already in progress on an engine that would add real sparkle to the new two-seater's performance.

Both Curtice and Keating were impressed with the car and Earl's enthusiasm for the project. Construction of a prototype for display at the company's 1953 Motorama shows was sanctioned immediately, the final decision on production depending very much on the car's reception at those shows. However, to be ready to put the car into production for 1953, should reaction be positive, detailed engineering work was carried out while the show car was being prepared. The name of the new sportscar was to be Corvette; little did its creators realize that in the decades to come that name would signify an automotive legend.

The first Motorama show of 1953 took place in New York, in January, and the Corvette was a runaway success. As the show progressed to other venues across the country, Chevrolet were bombarded with enquiries about the sportscar. Everybody wanted to know when it would be available and how much it would cost. In the face of such overwhelming enthusiasm, GM wasted no time in putting the car into production. And while the decades have seen considerable mechanical and styling changes, it has remained America's only true production two-seat sportscar.

Although the road has sometimes been a rocky one, the Corvette has endured for 40 years, offering value-for-money performance that is second to none.

BELOW: Four generations of Corvette from the '53 (left) to the '86 (right).

CHAPTER 1
The Classics

Remarkably, for a concept car, very little was changed when the Corvette was put into production later in 1953. Most of the changes were details, but the overall appearance and mechanical specifications were much the same as those of the Motorama Corvette that had captured the imagination of the millions of show-goers who had seen it. The first production version rolled off the factory line on 30 June that year.

What had excited so much attention was a sportscar unlike any produced in America before. The lightweight, two-seat GRP body was long and low, and was remarkable for several features. At the front, an oval grille opening was framed in chrome and filled with a row of vertical chromed 'teeth.' To each side of the grille was a recessed headlamp protected by a mesh stone-guard, below which was a tiny bumperette that was shaped to fit against the body. To the rear of the pancake-style hood was a wrap-around panoramic windshield, while behind the cockpit, a hinged panel concealed a cloth folding-top. The rounded profile of the rear fenders was interrupted by 'rocket-ship' tail fins carrying the rear lights, and the rear extremities of the fenders were protected by bumperettes that mirrored the style of those at the front. Other notable features at the rear were the recessed license plate that was mounted behind a

clear plastic 'window' and the tips of the exhausts that protruded through the rear panel.

Inside, there were bucket seats, a large-diameter, almost upright, steering wheel with a central chrome horn-ring, a large, semi-circular speedometer and a comprehensive collection of instruments strung out across the dashboard. The interior also featured an optional heater, something that many imported sportscars didn't have.

Although, externally, the Corvette bore no resemblance to any other Chevy, under the skin much would be familiar to anyone who knew the division's standard fare. The chassis, however, was new, dictated by the wheelbase that had been chosen (102in.) and the positioning of the engine and cockpit relative to the back axle in an attempt to obtain equal weight distribution front and rear that would promote good handling. Built on traditional lines, the chassis had box-section side rails that were prevented from twisting by a large X-section crossmember in the center.

At the front, independent suspension (comprising unequal-length wishbones, coil springs, telescopic shock absorbers and a stabilizer bar) mirrored that found in the Chevrolet sedans of the day, although because of the lighter weight of the sportscar, the ratings of the various components were lower. Steering was also familiar, being a

ABOVE LEFT: The Corvette made quite an impact when it was introduced in 1953. No major American car manufacturer had produced anything like it. Its racy lines were in stark contrast to Chevrolet's bulbous, sedate family sedans.

LEFT: The two-seater roadster body was long and low – and made from fiberglass, another first for a major manufacturer.

RIGHT: The headlights were recessed into the tops of the fenders and protected by wire stone guards, while the oval grille contained a row of chromed 'teeth.'

LEFT: At the rear, 'rocket ship' fins carried the lights, while the license plate was recessed into the trunk lid behind a clear plastic window. The exhaust tips protruded through the rear panel and the bumper was a three-piece item fixed directly to the body.

RIGHT: All '53 Corvettes came in white with a red interior. A tiny selector lever for the Powerglide automatic transmission protruded from the transmission tunnel and the large-diameter steering wheel was nearly vertical.

BELOW LEFT: Unfortunately, when Chevrolet decided to build the Corvette, they didn't have a suitable engine for a sports car and wouldn't have for a couple of years. Thus, the tried and tested 'stovebolt' six was used. Triple Carter carburetors and other modifications boosted output to 150bhp.

Saginaw box with recirculating ball. At the rear, the rigid axle was carried on leaf springs, controlled by telescopic shock absorbers and mounted to the outside of the chassis rails for stability. Power was passed to the axle by an open drive shaft – a first for Chevrolet – and drum brakes were fitted to all four wheels.

Because of the expected low production run, there was no possibility of developing an engine specifically for the Corvette; the only option was Chevrolet's tried and tested 235cu.in. inline six, as used in the sedans, but hardly an obvious choice for a sportscar, being rated at 105bhp. So Chevy engineers set to work to give it some more 'get up and go.' This they did by modifying the cylinder head to bump the compression ratio from 7.5:1 to 8.0:1 and slotting in a new camshaft, solid valve lifters and dual valve springs. The engine's breathing system received a complete revision with triple Carter side-draught carburetors and a special dual exhaust arrangement. To clear the low hoodline, the valve cover was reworked at the front end to give it a flatter profile. The modifications produced another 45bhp.

The transmission of the new Corvette came in for considerable criticism from sportscar buffs; it was not the manual device they considered essential for any car of its type, but rather another item from the Chevrolet stock list – the Powerglide two-speed automatic. On reflection, it does seem a strange choice indeed for a car with such sporting aspirations, but there was nothing else suitable on the shelves, nor were there the time or resources to develop a suitable manual transmission. The Powerglide was tough and uncomplicated and would do the job; at least it was controlled by a floor-mounted shifter which, if nothing else, looked the part.

It was in this form that Chevrolet completed 300 examples of the Corvette in 1953. All were finished in Polo white with Sportsman red interiors and black folding-tops, matching the Motorama prototype.

In general, the Corvette was well received by Press and public alike even though the automatic transmission came in for adverse comment. The car performed well, however, (it was capable of 0-60mph in around 11 seconds and could top 100mph with ease) and was praised for its ride and road-holding. There were a few niggles, such as the side curtains for use with the top in adverse weather. There were also no exterior door handles, so it was necessary to reach inside to open the door, a maneuver made all the more difficult by the side curtains.

LEFT: There were few obvious changes to the Corvette for 1954, although power output of the inline six was bumped by another 5bhp. This example is finished in the original white scheme, but other colors were offered that year in an attempt to boost sales.

RIGHT: The folding top was concealed beneath a hinged panel behind the cockpit when not in use. Early models of 'vette had clip-on side screens that were far from popular.

BELOW: Particularly unsportscar-like were the full-size wheel covers complete with dummy knock-off spinners – at the time, genuine knock-off wire wheels would have been expected by most sportscar buffs. However, Corvettes would continue with these wheel trims for a long time.

When the 1954 model arrived, there was not much that was obviously different, although lots of minor changes were made throughout the year to make the car better. One obvious difference was the fact that the car could be had with a Pennant blue or Sportsman red paint finish in addition to white; the former had a tan interior, while the other two had red interiors. A few cars were painted black. A new camshaft was also fitted that boosted power to 155 bhp.

As 1954 drew to a close, however, the Corvette was in big trouble. Despite all the fine words in the Press and the ex-cellent reception at the Motoramas, the car simply wasn't selling. In all 3600 Corvettes had been built for 1954, and by the time the '55 model was ready, almost half of them were still unsold. Sadly, the Corvette fell between two stools: it was too gimmicky for the real sportscar buff and too uncomfortable for the country club set. Moreover, GM had failed to take note of the fact that the sportscar market as a whole was small; there was no way that they would sell 'vettes in the sort of numbers they were used to with their run-of-the-mill sedans.

Things got better – and worse – in 1955. Although outwardly the car remained unchanged that year, it received a massive shot in the arm performance-wise with the advent of Chevrolet's 265cu.in. overhead-valve V8. Developed by Chevy's chief engineer, Ed Cole, the smallblock V8 was to prove a major turning-point in the division's fortunes and was to put it in the performance market that previously had been dominated by arch-rivals Ford.

In the Corvette, the V8 developed 195bhp at 5000rpm and would push the lightweight roadster from rest to 60mph in 8.5 seconds, with a top speed not far short of 120mph. Furthermore, it did this while burning less fuel than the six; the V8 was even lighter than the old inline engine. Consequently, practically all the 'vettes built that year were ordered with the new engine. Unfortunately, a total of only 700 cars was ordered. A disaster indeed.

It looked like the end of the road for America's only production sportscar, but the cavalry arrived in the nick of time – in the shape of Ford's Thunderbird. Introduced in 1955, Ford's two-seater went on to sell over 16,000 copies that year, and Chevrolet weren't about to take that lying down. It was decided to keep the Corvette in production and use it to deny Ford that particular segment of the market.

Although, with the new V8, performance of the Corvette had been improved dramatically – aided by the introduction of a three-speed manual transmission toward the end of the '55 model run – the car's styling needed updating and all of the many niggles attending to. Luckily, Harley Earl had been working on the problem and a restyled Corvette was to appear in 1955 which was a considerable improvement on the old car.

Although firmly based on the old body style, from every angle the new 'vette looked different. At the front, the headlights had been pulled forward and the stone-guards dispensed with; the oval grille with its vertical 'teeth' remained, but the bumperettes were simplified considerably. At the back, the 'rocket-ship' fins were no more, the fenders being allowed to curve gracefully downwards, while the rear lights were set into their top edges. The exhaust outlets had been moved to the fender extremities and lengthened to prevent exhaust gases from being sucked into the cockpit, while the license plate was now mounted on a simple bracket in the center of the rear bumper.

A smart lift-off hardtop was made available, and to everyone's relief the clip-on side curtains were no more. Instead, the '56 Corvette had roll-up windows (with a power option); there were even exterior door handles. The sides also had a unique feature: a tapering, concave depression ran back from the front wheel wells to a point almost three-quarters of the way across the door and was outlined with a chrome trim. These body side 'coves,' as they were known, could be finished in a contrasting color to the main body.

On the whole, the design was far less fussy than the earlier cars and was only marred by the two scoops that were molded into the tops of the front fenders. These, originally, had been intended to provide cowl ventilation, but the extra cost ruled out the idea and so the scoops were made non-functional.

LEFT: For 1956, the body was restyled, which improved its looks considerably. The rounded rear end remained, but the rocket fins were dropped and the license plate now sat in the middle of the bumper centrepiece.

BELOW LEFT: Chevrolet's chief engineer, Ed Cole, was responsible for developing the small-block V8 that was to inject real performance into the 'vette for 1955.

RIGHT: Externally, the '56 and '57 models are indistinguishable. The oval grille of the original was retained, but the headlights were pulled forward to bring the styling up to date.

BELOW: Concave body side 'coves' gave the car more style, while a hardtop and roll-up windows provided far greater comfort than before.

LEFT: The checkered flag in the Corvette emblem would always indicate the sporting nature of the car.

FAR LEFT: Zora Arkus-Duntov played a significant role in the Corvette story over many years. His skill and enthusiasm would ensure that the 'vette would become an ever-stronger performer.

RIGHT: Instruments, other than the speedometer, were spaced out across the dashboard and not always easy to read.

BELOW: The '56 and '57 models were good-looking cars from every angle.

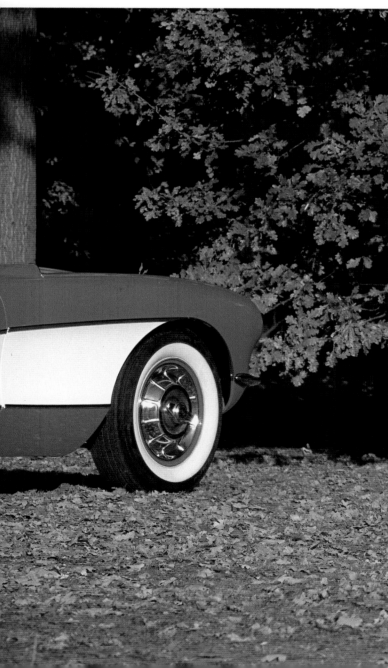

The Corvette now could only be had with the smallblock V8 engine which came in a 210bhp version with single four-barrel carburetor or as a 225bhp motor with special cams and dual four-barrels. The cams had been designed by a German-born engineer who would play a major part in the Corvette story as the years rolled by; his name was Zora Arkus-Duntov.

The three-speed manual gearbox was offered as standard equipment, with the Powerglide automatic as an option. Equipped with the former, the latest model of the Corvette could reach 60mph in 7.5 seconds. Mechanically, the rest of the car was very much as before, although several components were suitably strengthened to cope with the extra power of the V8.

By now, the Corvette was beginning to make a name for itself on the race track; Chevrolet themselves developing several machines purely for racing under the guidance and encouragement of Duntov. He firmly believed that track successes would lead to increased sales, and the division made much of the car's successes in their advertizing. Moreover, components developed to improve performance for racing would find their way on to the production cars, leading to an even better sportscar.

In terms of styling, the 1957 cars were virtually identical to those of the year before, but under the hood things could be quite a bit different. For a start, the engine had been opened up to 283cu.in. and it could be specified with a variety of equipment to give varying power outputs. In standard form, with a single four-barrel carburetor, it produced 220bhp, but there were dual four-barrel options that developed either 245 or 270bhp. The really big news, however, was that the '57 Corvette could be ordered with fuel injection; with this, the engine could be made to pump out 283bhp – 1 bhp per cu.in., something Chevy engineers had been striving to attain for some time and which gave the division something else to shout about in their advertizing.

LEFT: The body side coves could be emphasized by being finished in a contrasting color to the main body. In 1957 the sporty styling was complemented by the availability of fuel injection which allowed the 283cu.in. motor to develop 283bhp – the magic 1 bhp per cu.in.

BELOW LEFT: For 1956-57, the exhaust tips were moved to a more favorable position in the rear edges of the fenders.

BELOW: In many ways, the '56 and '57 models are the best looking of the 'classic' Corvettes. The front-end styling is just right, forming a distinct 'face,' and the overall styling makes a homogenous whole.

The fuel-injection system was another of Zora Arkus-Duntov's achievements and while it did suffer in terms of re-liability – and it was an expensive option – it made the 'vette that little bit extra special.

Another improvement on the '57 models was the avail-ability of a four-speed manual transmission which, with a range of optional rear axle ratios, made it possible to get the most from the available power. And that power made the Corvette a force to be reckoned with on both road and track. The acceleration of the 283bhp cars was incredible – one road tester recorded 0-60mph in 5.7 seconds. Top speeds were up too, at around 130mph. Uprated suspension and braking helped the Corvette cope with such figures.

There is no doubt that the 1956-57 models were a turning-point in the Corvette's fortunes after the disastrous sales figures of 1955. GM sold 6339 '57 models – fewer than they would have liked, it is true, but the figures were creeping upwards and the car was now the dual-purpose race/road car it always should have been.

Unfortunately, the 'race' portion of that description would now be played down as, along with other manu-facturers, GM agreed to a ban on all participation in racing. To the likes of Duntov and the many other 'vette enthusiasts within Chevrolet, this was criminal, but they soon managed to find ways round the ban and racing-orientated com-ponents continued to be developed unofficially. These were to make the Corvette an even more potent machine.

Toward the end of the Fifties, the trend in American car styling was for more glitz – fins appeared, along with lots of

chrome trim. It was the era of the jukebox on wheels. And
the Corvette came in for this treatment too, although it was
not as bad as some. For 1958, the clean design of the '56-'57
cars was cluttered with quad headlights, fake hood louvers,
large chrome-trimmed dummy air intakes on each side of
the grille, bigger bumpers, chrome strips across the trunk
lid and fake air vents in the side 'coves.' Inside, one definite
improvement was the grouping of all the instruments
directly in front of the driver – a long-awaited advance.

Although the restyling of the bodywork was thought by
many to have spoiled the package, in performance terms
there could be no complaints. Single and dual-carburetor
packages, plus fuel injection and different cams produced a
bhp range from 230 to 290. Despite the racing ban, there
was a long list of performance options to make the Corvette
race-ready, and the car was still making headlines on the
track, although Chevrolet couldn't acknowledge that fact.

The '58 models received a good press, and the public
liked the car, pushing the sales figures up once more. They
were up again in 1959 when the styling was cleaned up a
little by the removal of the fake hood louvers and trunk trim.
There were a few other minor changes, but the car was
essentially the same as the '58. Little was changed for 1960
as well, although the top-of-the-line engine, now with an
11:1 compression ratio, produced 315bhp.

At about this time, Harley Earl retired and was replaced
by Bill Mitchell, another of GM's Corvette enthusiasts and a
keen racer. Mitchell wanted to bring a breath of fresh air to
the 'vette with a completely new design, but cost con-
siderations ruled that out for the time being. Instead, he
managed to give the car a new look for 1961. In the main,
this involved restyling the rear end, making the fenders and
trunk blend into one homogenous shape, with dual rear
lights recessed into the rear panel.

The new rear-end treatment had come from Mitchell's

ABOVE: In 1961, the 'vette received a new rear-end treatment, while the headlight bezels were painted body color and the grille became a mesh insert.

LEFT: The interior remained the same, with the close instrument grouping and passenger grab rail.

ABOVE RIGHT: The 1961 model was the last available with a contrasting body cove color.

RIGHT: This '62 convertible features the radically redesigned rear end, with sharper styling.

OVERLEAF: '62 models no longer had the contrasting cove color, nor was it outlined with a bright trim.

Stingray racing car, a private project which had been based on the chassis of one of Duntov's Corvette-based racers from the days when Chevrolet were allowed to go racing. In fact, Mitchell received considerable 'back door' support from Chevy engineers, including Duntov, who were often to be seen around the pits at the race tracks. The Sting Ray's styling was to influence the next generation of Corvettes, too. In addition to the rear end, the body of the '61 received a mild cleaning up, with less chrome and a new expanded-mesh grille in place of the previous 'teeth.'

Mechanically, the car changed little, although the use of aluminum for several vital components produced a considerable weight saving which, in turn, produced performance gains. Even more performance was on tap in 1962, however, when the engine was bored out to 327cu.in. In standard form, it developed 250bhp, but this jumped to 360bhp if the top-of-the-range fuel-injected version was ordered. This had an 11.25:1 compression ratio, revised porting, special cams and solid valve lifters.

Externally, the '62 Corvette looked very similar to the previous year's car, but there was even less brightwork and the body side 'cove' could no longer be ordered in a contrasting color. This, the hottest performing 'vette so far, received plenty of praise in the magazines and it sold in sufficient numbers for Chevrolet to start making a profit on the car. The future was looking bright for America's only production sportscar and even better things from Corvette were just around the corner.

1959 Stingray Racer

Chapter 2
Enter the Sting Ray

Although they may not have realized it, as race fans watched Bill Mitchell's sleek, bright red championship-winning Stingray racer in the late Fifties and early Sixties, they were getting a privileged glimpse into the future, for the car's sharp-looking styling was to lead to a brand-new Corvette in 1963. That Corvette would carry the name 'Sting Ray.'

As GM's head of styling and one of the company's Corvette advocates, Mitchell brought considerable influence to bear on the new car. The 1962 models could trace their lineage back to the very first Corvettes of 1953, but now was the time for change, now was the time for styling that matched the car's impressive performance. When the Corvette Sting Ray was announced, it caused a sensation; Chevy couldn't build it quickly enough to satisfy the demand. The two-seat roadster had sharp, stylish good looks, but there was more – a beautiful fastback coupe.

The Sting Ray was a giant step away from the styling of the earlier Corvettes, producing a one-piece look that was totally up-to-date. No longer did the fenders appear to be separate appendages, but rather they were integrated into the overall shape of the car. At the front, there was a wide grille flanked by tiny round turn signals and partially concealed by large quarter bumpers. Above the grille, quad headlights were concealed by pivoting covers, giving the front end an uncluttered appearance. A large tapering bulge ran along the center of the pancake-style hood to the base of the windshield and on each side of it were depressions in the hood that carried fake cooling vents. Twin fake vents were also provided in the front fenders just behind the wheel wells.

At the rear, the styling was very similar to that of the '61-'62 models with recessed quad lights and the fenders sweeping round into the rear panel. However, unlike those earlier cars, there was no separate trunk lid and access to the restricted luggage area was from inside the car. The roadster had a folding top concealed beneath a hinged panel and there was the option of a lift-off hardtop.

The roofline of the coupe swept down toward the tail of the car, tapering to a point as it did so, while the door tops were actually cut into the roof. A unique feature of the first Sting Ray coupe was the split rear window, which was the

ABOVE LEFT: The Sting Ray of 1963 owed much of its dramatic styling to Bill Mitchell's Stingray racer and to the Mako Shark concept car which appeared in 1961. The rear end styling had already debuted on the Corvette of 1961, but the Mako Shark had many front-end features that were to appear in 1963 on the Corvette Sting Ray.

LEFT: Originally finished in bright red, Mitchell's racer appeared in the late fifties. Its styling is unmistakeably a forerunner of the 1963 'vette.

RIGHT: The Mako Shark was based on a Corvette roadster, although it was radically different. Exhaust headers protruded through the fenders and ran into mufflers mounted below the rocker panels. The emblem is appropriate.

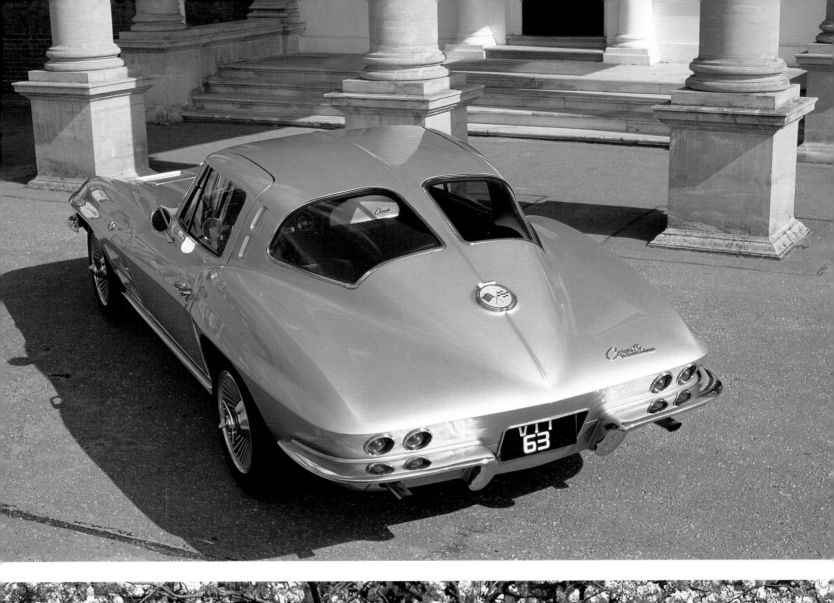

ABOVE LEFT: For the first time since the Corvette was introduced, a coupe joined the roadster. It was a striking design, made all the more striking by the controversial split rear window.

LEFT: The split-window 'vette is now the most sought after of the '63-'67 models, but at the time many were converted to one-piece windows. Mitchell insisted that it was an essential part of the design, but the press slammed it.

ABOVE: Apart from the similarity of rear-end styling, the '63 Sting Ray was unlike any Corvette that had gone before. The front end incorporated pop-up headlights – a Corvette trademark ever since.

RIGHT: The split rear window allowed a spine-like lip to run from just above the windshield to the tail.

LEFT: The '63 roadster was just as good looking as the coupe.

RIGHT: The rear deck carried the Sting Ray name, but no trunk lid.

BELOW LEFT: The headlight pods rotated to reveal quad lights.

BELOW: The dashboard placed all the instruments where they needed to be – directly in front of the driver.

cause of considerable comment at the time. There is no doubt that the divided rear window, which allowed a raised lip to run uninterrupted from the top of the windshield right down to the tail like a spine, gave the car an even more distinctive appearance. The more practical among the car's exponents argued that it detracted from the driver's rearward vision, but Mitchell insisted that it stay, saying that it was an essential part of the overall design.

Although he won the split-window argument for the '63 model, Mitchell had to concede defeat for subsequent versions of the coupe in the face of continual criticism from within GM and from the Press. Interestingly, the split window didn't seem to have any detrimental effect on sales of the fastback, which went like the proverbial hot cakes.

Both versions of the car were two-seaters (indeed, all Corvettes have been) and to go with the new body styles

were revised interiors. A pair of bucket seats was separated by a central console and transmission tunnel, while the dashboard incorporated two semi-circular cowls. On the driver's side, the cowl contained comprehensive instrumentation, while in front of the passenger seat there was a lidded glove compartment.

There was much that was new beneath the car, too, including the chassis, which was necessary not only because the wheelbase had been shortened to 98in., but also because of the extra loadings put upon it by the Duntov-designed independent rear suspension. This comprised a solidly-mounted differential with U-jointed halfshafts that were linked to the hub carriers. A control arm spanned between the base of the differential and the base of each hub carrier, while suspension was provided by a transverse leaf spring and telescopic shock absorbers.

LEFT: The cockpit was divided by a central console that merged into the deep transmission tunnel. In front of the passenger was a lidded glove compartment beneath a curved coaming that incorporated a hand-hold.

RIGHT: One of the few changes made for 1964 was the removal of the grilles from the hood depressions. That year also saw increases in engine horsepower – to 365bhp for the carbureted engine and 375bhp for the fuel-injected motor.

BELOW RIGHT: A major difference in the coupe's styling for 1964 was the installation of a one-piece rear window, which certainly improved rearward visibility.

BELOW: Detail of Corvette 327 turbo-fire. Introduced in 1970.

Suspension at the front was much as it had been on the earlier cars, as were the steering and the brakes. The last were still drums all around, but with wider linings to cope with the power developed by the car.

The engines and transmissions were those offered with the '62 Corvette: the former ranged from the 250bhp carbureted 327 through to a 360bhp fuel-injected unit, while the latter comprised the three-speed and four-speed manual gearboxes together with the two-speed Powerglide automatic. A variety of rear axle ratios was offered along with a Positraction limited-slip differential, while the options list included a range of performance-orientated parts. Among these were cast-aluminum knock-off wheels – a first for the 'vette which, hitherto, had been equipped with wheel covers that carried fake knock-off spinners and were often made fun of by the more snobbish of sportscar buffs.

Rear window criticisms aside, the Press loved the new 'vette, praising its ride and handling. Its performance was on a par with the '62 models, the fuel-injected versions being capable of the 0-60mph dash in under 6 seconds, while top speed was well over 130mph. With sales figures increased by half as much again on the '62 model, Chevy had a winner on their hands, not only on the road but also, whether they liked it or not, on the track.

For 1964 there were minor changes to improve the ride and sound insulation, while the engines offered a choice of

250, 300, 365 or 375bhp, depending on the specification ordered. The split rear window disappeared in favor of a one-piece unit.

As 1965 rolled around, the Sting Ray was really making its mark. That year, body modifications saw the hood depressions smoothed out and a set of functioning air vents let into

LEFT: The '64 roadster differed little from the '63 model. As with earlier 'vettes, its folding top was concealed beneath a hinged panel immediately behind the cockpit.

RIGHT: Few changes were made to the interior for 1965, although the door panel design changed, as did the seats.

BELOW LEFT: The 1963 Corvette Sting Ray roadster was in stark contrast to the first generation of Corvettes. Its sharp styling produced a purposeful, one-piece look.

BELOW: Externally, the '65 model lost the hood depressions and gained three functioning vents behind the front wheel. Side-mounted exhausts were also available as optional equipment.

the front fenders behind the wheel wells. There was also major news in the braking department with the announcement of four-wheel disc brakes that improved the car's stopping power considerably. Even when fitted with heavy-duty linings and finned drums to dissipate heat, the original brakes had already shown a propensity to fade under heavy use, but the disc set-up just kept on bringing the car to a rapid halt.

There is an old hot-rodder's axiom that says there's no substitute for cubic inches; in other words, if you want more performance, stuff in a bigger engine, and Chevy obviously felt that some of its customers wanted more than the 'vette's already impressive showing. Therefore, they made the '65 Sting Ray available with a 396cu.in. carbureted big-block V8 that produced an astounding 425bhp, uprating the running gear accordingly to cope with the extra power. When it was introduced, half-way through the model year, this engine replaced the 365bhp small-block unit. With the right gearing, this engine could produce a 0-60mph time of around 5.5 seconds and a top speed of over 150mph.

To clear the new big-block motor, it was necessary to form a large power bulge in the hood which, while it spoiled the lines a little, gave the car an even more purposeful appearance. This could be enhanced still further with another option introduced that year – side-mounted exhausts. These ran along the rocker panels, beneath the doors, and were shielded by perforated chromed guards.

ABOVE: The crossed flags were to remain a Corvette emblem for years to come.

LEFT: The rear deck script was relatively understated.

ABOVE RIGHT: Fuel injection was only available until the end of 1965 – it had proved too expensive and temperamental. Instead, Chevy followed the old adage that 'there's no substitute for cubic inches' and made available a 396cu.in. big-block motor that pumped out 425bhp.

RIGHT: The 1965 coupe and roadster were cleaner-looking cars due to the absence of the hood depressions.

LEFT: The '67 Sting Ray was put into production at the last minute, following problems with the next generation of Corvette. In many ways it is the cleanest of the '63-'67 models, being devoid of unnecessary frills.

RIGHT: The rear-end styling of the '63-'67 series changed hardly at all during that period, although a reversing light above the license plate was unique to the '67.

BELOW LEFT: As standard, the '67 was equipped with bolt-on 'Rallye' wheels. Even the optional vaned cast aluminum wheels were no longer knock-offs to meet federal legislation.

BELOW: Three 427cu.in. engines were available in 1967, rated at 390, 400 and 435bhp. A special hood with moulded-in scoop was developed to clear this engine and carried the engine size in large letters on each side.

Outwardly, the Sting Ray for 1966 looked very similar to the '65 model, but Chevy had been playing the cubic inch game again. This time the engine options comprised 250 and 350 bhp small-block 327s together with 390 and 427bhp 427cu.in. big-blocks. The last could propel the 'vette to neck-snapping sub 5 second 0-60mph times; not surprisingly, the specialist Press couldn't praise the car enough.

More news for 1966 was that fuel injection wasn't offered on any of the engine options; the level of performance de-livered by the carbureted versions was such that the added complication and expense were not warranted.

As 1966 slid by, Press and 'vette enthusiasts alike were anxiously awaiting the debut of the 1967 Sting Ray which everyone expected to be a restyled car. Indeed, that was the intention: GM had a new model Corvette in the wings, but, very late in the day, they decided to hold over production for another year. Unforeseen aerodynamic problems had caused considerable concern, such that it was decided not to launch the new car until they had been sorted out. As a result, the existing model was rolled out once more, still in roadster and coupe body styles, but generally tidied up compared to earlier versions.

In place of the hood bulge, there was a large air scoop for the 427cu.in. engines, of which there were three: 390, 400 and 435bhp. Two smallblock 327s were also available de-veloping 300 and 350bhp. In fact, there was a fourth 427 engine on the options list under the designation L-88, but this was a full-blooded (and expensive) competition engine that was capable of developing well over 500bhp. Very few L-88s were ordered, but its presence showed that, despite GM's official anti-racing stance, Duntov and his crew were still able to provide the means by which Corvettes could be made front-runners on the track.

The cleaned-up '67 Sting Ray received a very good press, not only for its still very impressive performance, but also because much of the gimmickry on the body had gone. The result was a very clean, if slightly dated, design. It was one that would go down in history among 'vette fans, many of whom consider it to be the best Corvette ever. It certainly was a tough act to follow, but as 1968 rolled near everyone was sure that the next model would be better still.

CHAPTER 3

The Mako Generation

Although GM's last Motorama show had taken place in 1961, the company continued to test public opinion to its styling ideas with one-off concept cars, which often gave a clue to what was to come. Sometimes the ideas never came to fruition, while at others (as had happened with the first Corvette) they found their way into production, albeit in watered-down form. In 1961, the company had shown a Corvette-based roadster called the Mako Shark. This incorporated elements of the design that eventually became the '63 Corvette, including the tapering hump across the hood, the full-width grille and the tail-end treatment. In 1965 the Mako II appeared, an altogether 'swoopier' car indeed. It had a low, wedge-shaped nose, voluptuous flowing fenders, a nipped-in center section and a tapering fastback roofline. When the new Corvette for 1968 appeared, there was no mistaking the inspiration behind its design; although slightly less radical in appearance, it was the Mako's offspring.

As the end of the Sixties approached, while sales of the Corvette were still good, it was under threat. This was the day of the 'ponycar,' so called because of Ford's phenomenal success with its GT car, the Mustang, which sparked off a blitz of similar sporty machinery, such as the Dodge Charger and GM's own Pontiac Firebird and Chevrolet Camaro. These cars appealed to the young, offering good looks and excellent performance at relatively low prices. There is no doubt that the 'vette was losing sales to some of these newcomers, so something radical was needed.

ABOVE: The '68 Corvette was a much shapelier car than the Sting Ray with voluptuous flowing fenders. Four functional air vents were incorporated behind the front wheel. This one has aftermarket American Racing wheels.

LEFT: The new 'vette was a completely different shape to the old one. However, the pop-up headlights remained a feature.

RIGHT: The flowing, waisted styling of the '68 Corvette certainly turned heads, although the Press were not too keen. One problem of the design was that it restricted shoulder room inside; another was that it required a much lower seat back angle because of the low roofline.

OVERLEAF: The coupe version of the new Corvette had removable roof panels and a 'duck-tail' rear spoiler. The rear roof pillars swept down to the tail, but the rear window was vertical.

In performance terms, the Corvette had nothing to be ashamed of, and the easiest solution was to wrap the existing hardware in a new set of eye-catching clothes. This Mitchell and his stylists did, basing the new body on the earlier car's 98in. wheelbase chassis.

The overall shape of the new Corvette was very reminiscent of the Mako II with the wedge-shaped nose (containing pop-up headlights) and flowing, rounded fenders. At the rear, the deck and rear panel met to form a spoiler lip that from the side gave the car a 'duck-tailed' look, while quad tail lights were recessed into the rear panel. The Mako had been a coupe, but the new Corvette came in both roadster and coupe styles. Unlike the Mako, the latter had an upright rear window framed by the rear roof pillars that tapered and flowed back into the deck. A unique feature of the roof was that it contained two removable panels above the passenger compartment so that the benefits of an open roadster and closed coupe could be enjoyed in one car.

Despite the fact that the new Corvette still produced astounding performance, particularly the big-block models, it came in for considerable criticism from the Press who slammed its swoopy looks and bemoaned the quality of finish, which had reached an all-time low. The styling had resulted in a narrower passenger compartment which was cramped still further by an enlarged transmission tunnel that was necessary to clear a new three-speed automatic transmission. The seats were laid back at a greater angle and none too comfortable, while the instruments were no longer grouped sensibly in front of the driver. The big-engined cars also suffered cooling problems.

Despite the year's delay in production, it was as if GM had rushed the new Corvette on to the market before it had had all the bugs ironed out. Even so, more people than ever before bought a Corvette in 1968 – 28,566 in total.

RIGHT: As usual, the Corvette for 1968 was available as a roadster as well as a coupe. This version has the standard 'Rallye' wheels. The raked windshield and shapely styling were to survive for many years, although these early models received a reputation of poor build quality that was not unjustified.

BELOW: Along with a new body style went a new interior, but the positioning of the auxiliary instruments could have been better.

BELOW RIGHT: The rear deck flowed into the ducktail spoiler lip, while the rear panel incorporated four recessed tail lights – another Corvette trademark. The folding top was concealed beneath a hinged panel, as before, and there was no trunk lid – you had to reach the trunk from inside the car.

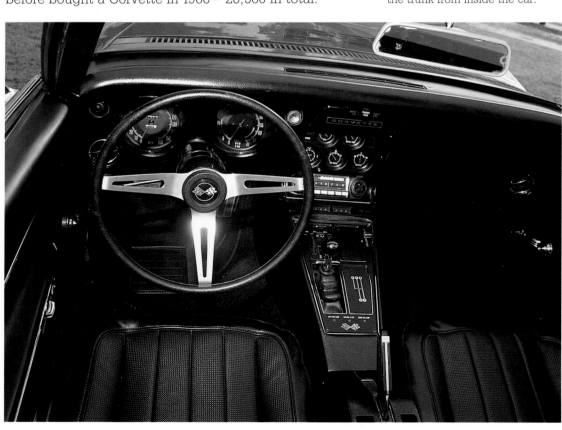

LEFT: There were few obvious changes for 1969, although the car was now called Stingray – note one word, not two as before. To meet criticisms of a lack of shoulder room inside, Duntov redesigned the door panels to make more room.

RIGHT: An option for 1969 was the side-mounted exhaust system, along with chrome trims for the front fender slots.

BELOW: In addition to having removable roof panels, the coupe also had a removable rear window to combine the benefits of a top-down roadster and the weather protection of a coupe. The wide tyres and wrap-under bodywork led to serious paint chip problems on both front and rear fenders.

BELOW RIGHT: Despite the drawbacks of the waisted body style, the new generation of Corvettes was to sell extremely well. In performance terms, they offered good value for money, and they were still America's only production sportscar.

When the new 'vette had appeared in 1968 it did so without the Sting Ray name, but for 1969 the name was back, although this time as one word – Stingray. Furthermore, that year's model had many of the criticisms of its predecessor attended to, including a redesign of the door panels to increase shoulder room inside.

The small-block engines were now bored out to 350cu.in, but were still rated at 300 and 350bhp, while the 427s remained as they were. By now, the need to meet government exhaust emissions requirements was having an effect on the powerplants, and for 1970 the options were fewer. The 350cu.in. small-blocks came in 330, 350 and 370bhp versions, while the 427s were dropped in favor of a 454cu.in. big-block that gave 390bhp.

Few body modifications were made between 1970 and 1972, by which time the engine options included a 330bhp small-block and 365 and 425bhp big blocks. For 1973, however, a major styling change was made to the front end of the car which received a deformable plastic nosepiece to comply with the requirement that all cars be fitted with a bumper that would absorb the impact of a 5mph collision. The nosepiece was a particularly neat solution to a problem which was solved on most other cars by the installation of a large, ugly matt black girder that did nothing for a vehicle's appearance.

With engine power output being reduced in the light of emissions requirements, the 350cu.in small-block was now rated at 190 and 250bhp, while the 454cu.in. engine was quoted at 275bhp. Even so, the Corvette still represented good value for money in terms of performance and it continued to sell well.

TOP: 1970 saw the availability of a 454cu.in. big-block motor.

ABOVE: A new front fender grille appeared in 1970, as did flared wheel wells to protect the bodywork from flying stones.

RIGHT: For 1973 there was a new hood and 'soft' front bumper.

LEFT: A luggage rack improves the roadster's limited trunk space.

ABOVE: The '73 Corvette was an interim model in that it had the 'soft' body-color 5mph front bumper and the standard chromed rear bumper. This was remedied in 1974 when a 'soft' tail piece was also added. This shot clearly shows how removing the roof panels from the coupe gave it a real open-car feel.

LEFT: Why the Sting Ray name of 1963-7 became Stingray for the Mako-influenced cars remains a mystery.

ABOVE RIGHT: In 1974, the Corvette received a body-color combined rear panel and 5mph bumper. The two-piece moulding gave the car a much more co-ordinated look.

RIGHT: The brace between the windshield frame and rear portion of the roof was necessary to stiffen the body when the roof panels were removed.

OVERLEAF: The new hood introduced in 1973 had a raised lip at the rear to conceal the windshield wipers. Previously, these had been hidden beneath a vacuum-operated panel.

LEFT: The swoopy styling of the Mako-based cars gave them a very muscular appearance. This example is a Silver Anniversary model, one of two special Corvettes offered in 1978.

RIGHT: The interior detail of the Mustang '78 Silver Anniversary model.

BELOW LEFT: The Silver Anniversary Corvette came in a two-tone silver-gray metallic finish with cast-aluminum wheels.

In 1974 the Stingray received a body-color plastic tail to match the front and this incorporated the Corvette trademark of four recessed tail lights, which were buried deeply in the rear panel. Although there were other changes, they were all of a minor nature.

By 1975, however, the Stingray's personality was showing distinct signs of change. Again to meet exhaust emissions requirements, the car was equipped with catalytic converters; the big-block engine was a thing of the past and there were only two small-block options – the base 165bhp motor and the 205bhp unit, both of which could only be run on unleaded fuel. Performance suffered accordingly, no more did the car produce neck-snapping acceleration; it had become a grand tourer. In terms of styling, too, there were few changes, although 1975 would be the last year that a roadster would be offered. From now on, the Stingray would be a coupe only, just like its Mako II forebear.

The formula stayed pretty much the same through 1976 and 1977, with refinements being made in terms of comfort and noise insulation. The Stingray name also disappeared from the 1977 model, never to be seen again.

Remarkably, despite the fact that the car still looked ostensibly the same as the '68 version, and offered far less in terms of performance, it sold in greater numbers than ever before; in all, 46,558 Corvettes were sold for 1977.

1978 marked the silver anniversary of the Corvette, and Chevrolet celebrated 25 years of production with a revised model of the coupe that saw the style return to a full fastback once more. In place of the tapering rear roof pillars and upright rear window was a large wrap-around rear window that gave the interior a much lighter, airier feel. Moreover, the lift-off roof panels could also be ordered in glass to improve the impression of spaciousness even further.

All Corvettes that year carried badges that proclaimed the silver anniversary of the car, and a special two-tone silver paint scheme was available as an option, together with a set of slotted cast aluminum wheels. Base engine for the '78 'vette was the tried and true 350cu.in. smallblock rated at 185bhp with a 220bhp version listed as an option. There was a choice of two four-speed manual gearboxes or a three-speed Turbo Hydramatic automatic.

Another special model available in 1978 was the Pace Car replica: that year a Corvette had been used as the official pace car for the Indianapolis 500, and Chevy made the most of the opportunity by selling copies to the public. The Pace Car replica featured spoilers at front and rear, cast aluminum wheels and a two-tone black and silver paint scheme, while the interior was finished in silver-gray. The car came with a set of decals proclaiming 'Official Pace Car' for the owner to add if he or she wished.

The Pace Car replica was a very striking-looking vehicle and some of its features were to be carried over on to subsequent models. In the following year, 1979, the bolt-on front and rear spoilers were offered as options on all models, which also received a new design of lightweight bucket seat that had made its debut in the Pace Car. For 1980, the spoilers were molded in as integral parts of the deformable plastic nose and tail pieces and were said to reduce aerodynamic drag, thus saving fuel.

In an effort to improve fuel economy still further, Chevy set about reducing the weight of the Corvette for 1980, using aluminum for the front chassis crossmember and differential housing, while both engine options had an aluminum inlet manifold. Weight savings were made in other areas, too, by the use of thinner GRP panels and glass.

That year the Corvette fan had a choice of 190 or 230bhp 350cu.in. small-block engines linked to either a four-speed manual gearbox or three-speed automatic transmission, unless he or she lived in California, in which case the only set-up on offer was a 180bhp 305cu.in. engine with the

automatic. Whatever the powertrain, it could easily push the speedometer needle off the dial, since it was only calibrated to 85mph in accordance with government requirements, but in the face of a 55mph maximum speed limit across the country, in theory that didn't matter.

By now, having been in production for 13 years, the Mako II-inspired Corvette was becoming a bit long in the tooth and once again rumors were flying around about the imminent arrival of a new 'vette. In fact, that car was still a couple of years away, but its presence meant that GM were not going to make any major or radical changes to the existing car, particularly as it was still selling extremely well. Indeed, the buoyant sales figures bore testimony to the soundness of the design.

Consequently, 1981 Corvettes were little changed from their immediate predecessors, although cars equipped with automatic transmissions were fitted with a special GRP rear spring that produced a weight saving of over 25lbs. All models that year were also fitted with a computerized emissions control system that ensured accurate fuel metering.

Body styling didn't change for 1982, either, although, this would be the last year that it would appear. The new Corvette would debut in 1983, and GM were using the '82 model to introduce the powertrain. This was still based on the familiar 350cu.in. small-block V8, but instead of a carburetor, this engine was equipped with a computer-controlled, twin-throttle-body fuel injection system that they called Cross-Fire Injection. The engine was rated at 200bhp and came linked to a new four-speed automatic transmission only. This package could push the car from rest to 60mph in just under 8 seconds.

To commemorate the fact that this was the last of the Mako generation, Chevrolet introduced a special Collector Edition of the '82 Corvette which was finished in a unique silvery-gold color with contrasting shadow stripes. Special emblems and cast aluminum wheels set it apart further from the standard cars, as did a unique feature – an opening rear hatch. The entire rear window was hinged to provide access to the luggage area, an extremely useful addition and something that would have benefited all the Corvettes since 1978 when the fastback-style, wrap-around rear window was introduced.

Much had happened to the Corvette in the previous 15 years, it had gone from a rip-snorting, asphalt-pounding street racer to a far more refined, less powerful grand tourer. One thing for sure was that its following was as strong as ever, and that following had very high hopes for the new generation of the car – they were not to be disappointed.

ABOVE: Second of the two specials offered in 1978 was the Pace Car replica, which commemorated the use of the Corvette as official pace car for that year's Indianapolis 500 race. With a silver and black paint scheme, silver interior and bedecked with spoilers, this special 'vette came with all the necessary decals to make it look like the real thing. Many owners chose not to apply them, but some did.

RIGHT: The Indianapolis Motor Speedway decal is authentic.

ABOVE: There were few styling changes in the years between 1978 and the end of the Mako cars in 1982. However, the nose and tail pieces were redesigned to incorporate the spoilers that, previously, had been separate components. This '82 coupe was equipped with the 'Cross-Fire Injection' computer-controlled fuel injection system.

LEFT: Albeit with some general smoothing out, the styling of the '82 Corvette is still clearly that of the '68 model – a 15-year run, which is not bad considering the criticism evoked by the design when it appeared.

RIGHT: The '82 Collector Edition celebrated 15 years of the Mako generation. It was offered with a special paint scheme and wheels, while the rear window became an openable hatch – something that would have benefited all 'vettes with that style of rear window.

CHAPTER 4
Getting Better All the Time

Traditionally, Chevrolet announces each year's new model in the September of the previous year, but in September 1982 no such new Corvette was announced for '83. There were rumors aplenty, of course, but nothing concrete until March when finally the new car did arrive, by which time it was listed as an '84 model. So, officially, there was no new Corvette for 1983.

Regardless of the year quoted, however, the 1984 Corvette was a stunner in many ways. It offered a package that contained superb performance and up-to-date styling that was still recognizably a Corvette thanks to the clever incorporation of several traditional features. Even so, although the powertrain was carried over from the previous model, the car was all new.

By now, the leading lights in the Corvette story – Bill Mitchell and Zora Arkus-Duntov – had long since retired from GM and their respective places in the Corvette program assumed by Jerry Palmer and David McLellan. The closest co-operation between these two and their design and engineering teams led to what was probably the most thoroughly integrated design ever in the history of the Corvette. Performance, handling, styling and passenger comfort were all provided to a high degree.

Whereas the cars of the previous 15 years had used effectively the same ladder-type chassis that had been introduced in 1963, the new 'vette was based on a completely new arrangement that provided a stiffer, but lighter, structure and was a partial move toward unitary construction. The main element in the new frame was a C-section steel pressing that acted as a 'backbone,' running down the center of the car. To this was welded an assembly of panels that formed a framework around the passenger compartment, framing the windshield and door openings and providing a rigid rear bulkhead. Subframes were attached to the framework to carry the engine, front suspension and steering, and the back bumper. The drive shaft passed down the center of the C-section backbone to the differential which was bolted rigidly to the rear.

Independent rear suspension was still the order of the day, but the Corvette's original arrangement had been considerably redesigned, with extra longitudinal and transverse links to the hub carriers. It still sported the GRP leaf spring, and a similar transverse leaf spring was now incorporated in the front suspension – running between the two lower wishbones – instead of the previous coil springs. The use of these springs produced a considerable weight

LEFT: The new shape Corvette was very different to its predecessor, and yet it wasn't. All the traditional Corvette styling clues were there, including the pop-up headlights. The swoopy, waisted design was no more, however, and the car was considerably wider, providing plenty of room inside. Despite the badging, there could be no doubt that this was a Corvette, no matter from what angle it was viewed.

RIGHT: Along with the new body styling came a 'Buck Rogers' style instrument panel with digital and graphic displays.

saving, and they were also said to have a longer life than conventional steel springs. Also new at the front was rack-and-pinion steering in place of the old recirculating-ball arrangement; it was power assisted as standard.

Four-wheel ventilated disc brakes handled the stopping chore, and the wheels themselves were a new cast-aluminum design, having wider rims at the rear than at the front. Moreover, the wheels were handed because of their integral brake cooling slots, so it was not possible to swop them from side to side.

Power for the package came from the Cross-Fire Injection 350cu.in. smallblock V8, as used in the '82 Corvette, although minor changes had boosted output by 5bhp to 205bhp. There was no alternative to the base engine, nor would there be for some years to come.

Behind the engine was a new four-speed manual gearbox, but this incorporated a computer-controlled overdrive facility that operated on all forward gears other than first. Its purpose was to improve fuel consumption at part-throttle settings, but it was automatically disengaged when the throttle was opened wide; an override switch was also provided for the driver. As an option to this transmission, there was the four-speed automatic that had been offered with the '82 Corvette.

This mechanical package was clothed in a GRP body that was completely new, yet bore some unmistakable Corvette features, so that there was no doubting the car's identity. In general terms, the body had a much less radical appearance than before; gone were the curving, humped fenders and the sucked-in mid-section, while the corners and angles were not as sharp. The body was smaller, too, although this was not immediately obvious. The car's wheelbase was reduced by 1¾in. and both front and rear overhangs were cut to give a body that was nearly 9in. shorter than before. It was slightly wider, however, and a substantial increase in shoulder width inside was achieved.

At the front, what had been twin air intakes were replaced by driving lights, cooling air for the radiator being taken from beneath the car. The nose was less pointed than before, but the pop-up headlights were still there and instead of one large power bulge running down the hood, there were two. The hood itself was blended into the fenders so that there was no obvious point where one began and the other ended, and the entire assembly opened clamshell-style to provide excellent access to the engine and accessories.

The belt-line ran back from the tops of the front fenders, across the doors to the rear fenders with no significant dip, as there had been on the earlier cars, thereby continuing the homogenous design. A very steeply-raked windshield was complemented by a tapering glass fastback rear window, much like that of the earlier car and hinged to provide access to the luggage compartment. The entire roof section above the seat was removable as one panel, continuing another Corvette tradition.

One more trademark was to be found at the rear where four round tail lights were deeply recessed into the notched rear panel. Something that was new, however, was the continuous rubbing strip that ran right around the center of the car, being broken only by the front and rear wheel wells. Not

LEFT: Despite the new looks, the engine was familiar, being the 350cu.in. smallblock with Cross-Fire Injection from the '82 Corvette. This remained the standard engine for some time to come.

ABOVE RIGHT: A shorter wheelbase and reduced front and rear overhangs produced a car that was 9in. shorter than its predecessor. Close co-operation between design and engineering departments ensured that the new 'vette was a very cohesive package indeed.

RIGHT: The front fender vents and recessed tail lights are standard Corvette features and confirm the identity of the post '82 cars.

LEFT: In the new Corvette, what would have been air intakes are now occupied by fog and turn signal lamps, while cooling air is taken from a point lower down.

RIGHT: This time, Chevrolet produced a body that was stiff enough to have the entire roof panel removed without causing problems.

BELOW RIGHT: The car underwent few significant styling changes between its introduction in 1984 and this 1987 model. The only obvious difference is the central stop light mounted to the roof of this coupe.

OVERLEAF: A rubbing strip runs around the entire car, providing a useful accent that conceals the opening line of the clamshell hood.

only was the whole package an attractive one, but it also ensured improved driving visibility and produced less aerodynamic drag than the previous cars.

To match the new look was a new interior that provided the occupants with more leg, head and shoulder room than before. The individual high-back bucket seats were separated by a deep center console/transmission tunnel, while all the instruments were grouped directly in front of the driver. The instruments themselves were space-age electronic units, giving both digital and graphic displays.

When the new Corvette arrived, the Press heaped it with praise for its leech-like roadholding and sub 7 second 0-60mph acceleration times. There were few production sportscars that could outperform the 'vette, particularly in cornering ability. However, that surefootedness also brought with it a drawback that the Press were quick to criticize. The ride was harsh because of the very stiff springs and, on all but the smoothest of surfaces, it made the Corvette quite uncomfortable compared to its predecessors. The 'Buck Rogers' instrument panel also came in for its fair share of detractors who found it unnecessarily complex and, in certain situations, difficult to read. Despite the niggles, Chevrolet produced 51,547 of the 1984 Corvette, proof that the model was fit to carry on the legend.

In terms of appearance, there was little to distinguish the 1985 Corvette from the previous year's model, but under the hood there was a change to the engine's induction system with a new multi-port fuel injection arrangement known as Tuned Port Injection. This allowed the 350cu.in. engine to develop an additional 25bhp, pushing the car to a 150mph top speed.

Work was also carried out on that year's model to improve the ride in the light of criticism of the '84 Corvette; spring rates were reduced, which helped matters, but generally the ride was still too harsh for many customers. Improvements to the car's ride would continue to be made for the next couple of years.

The big news for 1986 was the return of the Corvette roadster, which sold alongside the coupe. Body styling remained essentially the same, the roadster having a manually-operated folding-top concealed beneath a hinged panel, as of old. Because of the lack of a roof, much work was done on the open car to improve its stiffness. Additional bracing members were added to the chassis, while the rear bulkhead was strengthened. As a result of all this work, the roadster had far fewer rattles than the coupe. Consequently, the latter received the same modifications a year later.

A bright yellow example of the new Corvette roadster had been used as pace car for the Indianapolis 500 that year, and Chevrolet capitalized on this by referring to all the convertibles built – regardless of color – as Pace Car replicas, supplying them with the appropriate decals for application by the owner. Unlike the previous Pace Car replica, there was no difference in their level of equipment.

Few changes were made to the specification of the car in 1986, but in 1987 engine power was increased to 240bhp. This was due to an improved design of aluminum cylinder head and the use of roller valve lifters to reduce friction. That year also saw the availability of a twin-turbocharger-equipped version of the standard engine assembled outside GM by Calloway Engineering, but included in the standard

LEFT: The very business-like interior is split into two by a deep transmission tunnel and centre console.

RIGHT: Chevrolet had dropped the roadster from the Corvette line-up in 1976, but for 1986 they reintroduced the soft-top in the new body style.

BELOW RIGHT: With the headlights raised, the Corvette has a very distinct, almost comical, 'face'.

Corvette option list. This engine developed 345bhp and came as part of a complete performance package that resulted in a car capable of reaching 175mph and doing the 0-60mph sprint in substantially less than five seconds – shades of the golden days of Corvette performance.

For 1988 engine output was raised to 245bhp on the coupe by virtue of a revised exhaust system, while on both cars alterations to the suspension geometry improved stability under braking. There were also larger-diameter brake discs and a new design of cast aluminum wheel that year, again being handed left and right because of the direction of the brake cooling slots. There were no other obvious differences in this, the 35th anniversary year of the Corvette, but a special anniversary edition of the car was offered, being finished in white with a black band across the roof.

Racing has always played a big part in the Corvette's development over the years, often clandestinely, and the road-going cars have always benefited from developments for the track. Many modifications built into the standard cars by Chevy engineers during the late Eighties came as a result of competition experience. The advent of a six-speed manual gearbox in the 1989 Corvette was just such a race-inspired improvement. By then, the Sports Car Club of America was running a Corvette Challenge and the existing four-speed manual box was seen as a weak link in the car. Consequently, Chevrolet collaborated with the German transmission specialists Zahnradfabrik Friedrichshafen who were well known for their ZF competition gearboxes. The result was a six-speed unit with a computer-controlled lock-out on 2nd and 3rd gears for good fuel economy.

Another new item for 1989 was a removable hardtop for the roadster, echoing a feature from the past. A fresh seat design also appeared. Otherwise, things continued much as they were; the Corvette offered excellence in all things, so why change for the sake of it? But there was a change on the way, one which would set Corvette fans on their ears.

The Calloway Corvette option had continued through 1989 and into 1990, but that year also saw the debut of an even more ferocious Corvette. This was obtainable by ordering the ZR1 package. Developed in conjunction with English sportscar builders (but GM-owned) Lotus Cars, the ZR1 was powered by an all-new aluminum 350cu.in. V8 engine with double overhead camshafts and four valves per cylinder. Along with the engine came a reworked body that was stylishly flared at the wheel arches to cover wider tires and had a new rear panel. The ZR1 offered phenomenal performance in a sophisticated package, continuing the theme of the Corvette as dual-purpose race/road car – and at a relatively reasonable price.

The advent of the ZR1 put the Corvette right among the very best sportscars in the world – it is still America's only production sportscar and it is legendary. From the roadsters of the early Fifties, through the muscular Sting Rays of the Sixties and the grand tourers of the Seventies and Eighties, to the sophisticated coupes and roadsters of the Nineties, the Corvette has always offered excellent value for money in terms of performance and styling. It has held its own against a plethora of foreign competition and gathered a following that will always be loyal.

As the year 2000 approaches, it is difficult to imagine that the Corvette won't continue into the next century, continuing the excellence it has become famous for. The 50th anniversary model has to be a real winner.

LEFT: Although there is little to distinguish it externally, the Corvette ZR1 introduced in 1990 packs a powerful punch. Its all-aluminum, double-overhead-cam 350cu.in. V8 was developed in conjunction with English sports-car builders Lotus.

BELOW: The bodywork of the ZR1 features subtly flared wheel wells together with a redesigned tail piece with the familiar recessed quad tail lights. The car's awesome performance is belied by its relatively mild appearance and the refinement of the package is such that it rates among the best in the world.

Index

Page numbers in *italics* refer to illustrations

ACKNOWLEDGMENTS

The author and publisher would
like to thank David Eldred for
designing this book, Stephen
Small for the picture research and
Ron Watson for the index. The
following individuals and
agencies provided photographic
material:

Brompton Books, pages: 1(Bob
    Baldridge), 2-3, 14(bottom left),
    16(top left), 59(Bob Baldridge),
    60(Bob Baldridge).
Neill Bruce, pages: 12-13(all
    three), 40-41(all three), 42-43,
    50(bottom/Nicky Wright), 51(top/
    Nicky Wright), 52-53(Nicky
    Wright), 66-67(Nicky Wright).
Colin Burnham, pages: 18-
    19(all three)

Mike Key, pages: 4-5, 6-7,
    8-9(all three), 14(top), 14-15,
    15(top), 16(top right), 17(top),
    20-21(all five), 23(bottom), 26-
    27(all three), 28-20(all four), 30-
    31(all four), 32-33(all four),
    35(both), 36(top), 37(both), 38-
    39(all four), 44-45(all three),
    46(bottom), 47(top), 48-49(all
    five), 50(top), 51(bottom), 54-
    55(all three), 56-57(both), 58-

59(both), 61, 62-63(all three),
    68-69(all three).
Don Morley, pages: 64(top),
    65(top).
**National Motor Museum,
    England, pages:** 22(top/Nicky
    Wright), 22(bottom), 23(top),
    24-25(Nicky Wright), 34(both),
    36(bottom), 46(top/Nicky
    Wright), 47(bottom/Nicky
    Wright), 70(both/Nicky Wright).